Spiritualism My Way of Life

I0171418

Friends, Family & Associates,
I'm Not Crazy
What Happened Is – I Changed!

Reverend Bonnie Darby

ISBN: 978-0-578-15211-0

Published by: Reverend Bonnie Darby
d/b/a Conscious Awareness Living

Printed by CreateSpace.com, An Amazon Company
Available from Amazon.com, CreateSpace.com, and
other retail outlets

DEDICATION

To my church family who radiate the spirit of love that exists within The Spiritualist Church of Indianapolis I thank you for inspiring me!

ACKNOWLEDGMENT

Without the moral support and editing skills of my dear friends, this booklet would never have happened. Thank you! I want to acknowledge Mermaid Moon Productions who had the daunting task of getting me to sit still for a photograph. Great job!

CONTENTS

Preface

PREFACE

Spiritualism is not a well-known, nor a well understood religion. It is generally thought of as a cult. Synonyms for cult are often described as trendy, offbeat, alternative, unusual, fad, craze, sec, faction, religion, e.g. Yes, Spiritualism may fall under some of those categories but it is neither bizarre nor weird. My goal in writing this booklet is to help Spiritualism of today be appreciated for the good it serves to mankind. As a Pastor of The Spiritualist Church of Indianapolis (www.TSCOI.org), I converse with lots of people wanting to know more about the Science, Philosophy and Religion of Spiritualism. College students' call asking to attend services as part of their class work in religious studies; this booklet is from my own spiritual journey offering insight into my perception of Spiritualism and my life as a Spiritualist.

"Each morning we are born again. What we do today is what matters." ~ Buddha

WHY I BECAME A SPIRITUALIST

I am an Ordained Spiritualist Minister through the National Spiritualist Association of Churches (NSAC), Lily Dale, New York. I have been a Spiritualist for over twenty years. I am also a daughter, a sister, a widow, a mother, a grandmother and a great-grandmother. There is nothing outstanding about me or unusual or cultish. I am an average person just like you living a life and part of my life is the Religion of Spiritualism. Spiritualism transformed my life from the inside out. I like to say Spiritualism found me. In the way the Universe works it seems at a point in my life I started meeting this fascinating group of people who claimed Spiritualism as their religion. I had never heard of such a religion. I had however had dreams that came true, a near death experience and those wonderful gut feelings or intuitive inclinations. I did believe ghosts were a possibility but mostly the kind in books, movies or television.

When I walked into a Spiritualist Church I felt at home; and being a skeptic who spent most of my working years as a legal secretary everything had to be proven to my own standard of belief. I found there is more to Spiritualism than communicating with spirit entities. This included learning there are Natural

Laws of the Universe and realizing that you are in control of your life. I learned to respect all faiths and that everyone is exactly where they are supposed to be on their life journey as well as all spiritual beliefs and religions lead to a Higher Realm of existence in the afterlife. I learned that I Am one with Infinite Spirit and that the divine connection we all have never leaves us. Sometimes we may forget it's there but we are never separated from our Higher Power. I am not all knowing. I do not have all the answers, yet my twenty plus years as a Spiritualist taught me many things and a part of my journey is what I want to share with you.

As a Spiritualist my concept of the death and dying experience is more the theory of returning to our original form; it's simply discarding this physical body and living freely as a spirit in the Higher Realms. My husband died several years ago. I knew my husband feared the unknown of death. So as we embraced I told him to remember to look for the golden white light of God and follow the love energy into the light and that there would be spirit loved ones waiting for him. Those loving spirits would show him how everything worked on that plane of existence. I told him the spirits could be his mom, dad, son, brother, friends; or even his beloved dog Lady and that he would not be alone. After my husband made his transition, I went to a medium for a reading and was told my husband was with me. I will admit I thought, "Prove it" because the medium knew I was widowed. The message from my husband was basically that I was right in my beliefs about death and dying. The transition was much easier and his fears were groundless. Here again I admit I'm thinking this message was fluff and I needed proof that it was my husband. Then the medium very surprised said to me, "He is holding out a stick of black licorice". "Bingo" there was my proof! His favorite candy was licorice and the medium had no way of knowing this fact. The continuity of life has been proven to me again and again. As a medium, I have been blessed to connect with spirit loved ones for many people giving them peace of mind knowing our spirit never dies.

Spiritualism is about the continuity of life and so much more! When I chose Spiritualism as my belief system, it was partly because of mediumship and it was also about Natural Law and the realization that we are always in control of our life through our thoughts, words, deeds and actions. I learned everything is connected and everything is energy. I learned about living in the flow of the Universe. How this works is through the Laws of Nature which are the laws set in motion at the beginning of creation by our Infinite Spirit God. I learned that I did not have to feel like a tumble weed rolling through life randomly taking the bumps dealt me. I had choice and I was the one co-creating with the Infinite Spirit my future.

WHAT I BELIEVE AND WHY I BELIEVE

If I were asked what I believe how would I answer? I believe in a Higher Power, an omnipresent omnipotent force so magnificent that it is indescribable. There are many names used to identify this Magnificence – Spiritualists say Infinite Intelligence or Infinite Spirit or God or Holy Spirit. My mind sees a pulsating vibrating sparkling golden white light, a moving mass of energy and intelligence which is the Source of all that is and all that will ever be. All of creation emanates from this Source. Infinite Spirit set into motion the Laws of Nature wherein we exist and become co-creators. Somewhere, somehow within this Greatness is the Universal Consciousness of all that is known to exist and is ours to access and utilize. I believe there is a natural rhythm and flow to life itself. Synchronicity is a part of the flow and so are our own thoughts, words, actions and deeds. We are always connected to the Infinite Spirit and through our experiences the Infinite Spirit also learns and grows.

What set my belief in stone within me was a meditation experience. During this meditation I decided I wanted to visit God as an entity outside of myself and I was simply certain it was possible. Getting to God was a journey and there were experiences along the way but the awesomeness of the light of Infinite Spirit will always be part of me. I can't tell you if I was in a body or having an out of body experience – I was wholly there. Before me were ripples of golden white light streaming down from everywhere. I don't know if I saw them or sensed them. I only know in that moment it was real! From the ripples of light came a hand of light and this hand pressed my forehead with its palm. I could not even grasp the experience or have any understanding of what happened or what it meant. I became aware that I was back in my chair and I began to wonder could this have been real. Was this a vision or maybe a soul memory?

I was now full of questions – what did this mean – are there others with similar experiences? - am I crazy? I certainly didn't plan on telling anyone because I was sure my friends and family would find me certifiably crazy. There was also a dream that I had where I was hovering over light beings watching them move through a tunnel vortex into the light while I chanted "I am one with God and I will help many".

At this point in my life I was not a Spiritualist and I had no understanding of the significance of such experiences so they were put in the back of my mind because as awesome as these experiences were, I was entrenched in living my day to day life. Years passed and eventually some metaphysical books came to my attention. If memory serves me accurately, author James Van Praagh in his book "Talking to Heaven: describes his experience of seeing the hand of God and I realized I might not be so crazy after all. Throughout the years I came across more books telling of people's experiences and recollections of God. One book was "Memories of God and Creation – Remembering from the Subconscious Mind" by Sakuntuala Modi, M.D. where individuals during regression had similar recollections of the golden white light of God.

I wish I could tell you I became instantly enlightened by these early experiences but that would not be true. I was focused on raising children, working and doing all of life's important yet mundane activities, thus I chose to experience life on a more earthly level. Yes, it was a struggle at times with lots of learning going on. I can tell you that what I brought back from these experiences was that we are all the same, equal in the realms of Infinite Spirit.

So when I am asked what I believe – I believe in Infinite Spirit because I have experienced the golden white light and I believe there is so much more out there for us to understand.

TEACHINGS OF SPIRITUALISM

When I am asked what are the Teachings of Spiritualism this is my short version.

A belief in a Supreme Force or Power; this Supreme Force set into motion an orderly working of the Universe through Natural Law. The operation of Natural Law is why there is order and balance within all nature.

A belief in the continuity of life our consciousness, our spirit is immortal. We are a work in progress always evolving in the here and hereafter. Our existence in the hereafter has to do with our state of progression now and every soul can experience spiritual growth and enlightenment.

A belief in the phenomena of mediumship; wherein mediums working with and communicating with spirit entities prove that death is only of the physical body. Mediums and spirit healers working together for healings are simply channels for divine energy. Everything is of and from the Supreme Force.

A belief in personal responsibility; we create our existence through the operation of Natural Law. Therefore we are creating our existence with our thoughts, words, actions and deeds; this creation phenomenon will happen either randomly or consciously; the choice is ours.

A belief in the Golden Rule; and that its operation creates a harmonious existence for all!

INFINITE INTELLIGENCE/GOD

Spiritualism like all faiths has evolved into the beautiful religion we have today. I am a Spiritualist because it has proved to me my own immortality. I am a spirit living a human existence. To the never ending question do Spiritualists believe in God, the answer is "Yes"! We believe in an omnipotent, omnipresent, omniscient Higher Power and we humbly call this divine energy Infinite Intelligence, Infinite Spirit or God. I prefer Infinite Spirit because the concept is that our original form is spirit. We were made in the image of our creator. Thus being created in the image of our Higher Power and being spirit then it is logical that our creator is the Infinite

Spirit. As a Spiritualist I believe that the name is not important. I understand that man in earthly form may never fully comprehend the awesomeness of the Divine Source of all that is and all that ever will be.

I believe we are spirit first, a creation emanating from the Infinite Spirit – our spirit is our godliness and is eternal. Our spirit is who we truly are retaining our individuality and personality. We are spirit living in a human body made of solid mass/compressed energy – our bodies are a miraculous thing in its workings and functioning.

Infinite Spirit manifested spirits to experience, learn and grow. I believe we come from Infinite Spirit and we will ascend back to this Divine Source. God is love – God does not judge nor render punishment. The world is set in balance by Natural Law. We are working through our thoughts, words, actions and deeds constantly; and everything in our reality will rebalance itself either in this earth life or after our transition into the Higher Realms.

Destiny is not pre-destination. We may incarnate for a purpose or to experience or to learn a certain thing; we may incarnate to help another soul to have an experience such as patience; and on all levels of existence we have free will to move into any direction we desire. We limit ourselves – no one, no entity, nothing limits us but ourselves. We were given the free will to choose to be whomever we desire and experience life in the way we choose.

I don't think any two people have exactly the same belief in their Higher Power whether they are of the same faith or not. I think as we journey through life, we develop our personal belief in Infinite Spirit from our experiences. As an Ordained Minister I tell people, "What I share with you is my experience and education – I am not all knowing. I am a work in progress just like everyone else." I recommend every individual take what resonates within their heart and create their own truth and connection with Infinite Spirit.

RELIGION

Spiritualism teaches that *all* sacred books contain truths. No one text contains the absolute word. There is no right or wrong religion. Each is merely a different way of believing and guiding every individual to live to their highest and best. I believe everyone should form their own relationship with Infinite Spirit. I believe everyone is exactly where they are supposed to be in their life journey and faith system. If the Infinite Spirit had desired for all to believe and be the same then that would have been how we were created; rather than each of us searching for our own truth. I believe part of our life's journey on this earth plane is to be an expression of love and part of that expression is accepting diversity. There is no right or wrong concept. All belief systems are simply different paths leading to the Spirit Realms. Infinite Spirit is love and we are the expression of this love in the physical form. We should nurture that love and demonstrate it in all that we do and say.

As a Spiritualist I am often asked about my belief in Jesus the Christ. I believe in the teachings of Jesus. I believe Jesus was the son of Infinite Spirit just as we all emanate from this Divine Source. I believe Jesus braved the world and taught with passion the teachings within his heart of a way of right living and love. I do not see Jesus as a Savior God. I see Jesus as a great teacher and kindred soul. I do not believe the death of Jesus absolved me from my errors. I believe I am responsible for my choices as an operation of Natural Law and I will be working through the repercussions or rewards my choices bring. I believe Jesus existed and lived his life in greatness and I strive to pattern my life by the high ideals and teachings attributed to Jesus.

Our church services have a flow similar to most orthodox churches. Our service includes hands on healing where our healers are serving as channels for the healing energy of Infinite Spirit. We sing; instead of sermons we share a lecture and our speaker offers enlightenment for our life journey; we have invocations and benedictions; and we all share our bounty through offerings. What is special about a Spiritualist service is our demonstration of mediumship and an open appreciation of our mediums' diverse gifts. Our mediums give greetings from spirit loved ones proving the continuity of life.

Spiritualism teaches non-judgment. I do not believe the Infinite Spirit passes judgment and renders punishment when we transcend to the Higher Realms. I do believe we will continue to reflect on the lessons we have learned and the enlightenment we have garnered from our experiences, and continue our soul growth. The laws created by Infinite Spirit give us a system where there is no need for judgment. We as spirits will work out all facets of our journey through our own rebalancing.

Spiritualists believe that everyone is where they should be in life. Spiritualism does not evangelize or go out into the world for the purpose of converting souls; the Spiritualist faith allows the Universe to guide those who are seeking truth and enlightenment into our churches. Spiritualist churches do however promote and advertise allowing seekers to find our churches and camps. Our missionaries work diligently serving our churches or opening new churches where groups have gathered for this purpose.

Heaven and Hell are names given to places where some religions believe we spend eternity. I believe there are numerous planes of existence that are all at different rates of vibration from the lowest to the highest, and our spirit will gravitate to the plane of existence which best matches our own vibratory level at the time of transition. Our spirit retaining our personality continues to work and grow in the Higher Realms. We are an emanation of the Infinite Spirit. We continue our journey to raise our vibration so we can ascend back to our Divine Source from which we were created.

SPIRIT AND SPIRIT CHILDREN

Our first form is spirit. As spirit we are eternal beings existing in the likeness of our Source, Infinite Spirit. Before we incarnated in this physical body we were spirit and when this physical body dies we will continue our journey as spirit in the Spirit Realms.

As a Spiritualist I believe children in the Spirit Realms continue to grow. Their life on the earth plane may have been cut short by human standards but in a spiritual sense this earthly sojourn was only a small segment of their existence. This knowledge cannot alleviate the pain and suffering of missing their physical presence but it nurtures peace of mind. As a medium I have been privileged to give families some peace when messages come through from their loved one comforting them as tears of joy flow down their faces.

Why do I believe in the continuity of life? Because it has been proven to me through a near death experience and through documented near death experiences of many people. I remember very little of my own near death or out of body experience, and I've rarely talked to people outside of kindred souls about it. What I do remember is being outside of my body watching what was going on around me. At some point in the experience I remember looking at the clock. I was trying to ask the doctors and nurses what was going on, I wanted to know why there were so many people around my body. I asked what that person was doing with their fingers on the side of my neck. I remember wanting to know why everyone felt to be in such a high state of alertness. I became very frustrated because no one seemed to even hear me, no one answered my concerns. That's all I remember of my experience. When near death experiences became more mainstream I asked a friend who worked with hypnosis to regress me to the time of my near death experience so I could see if there was more to this incident but my friend refused. Her advice was basically I had made a choice to live out this life and I should leave it at that. What I gained from the experience is that we are so much more than our physical bodies.

DESTINY OR PRE-DESTINATION

My belief that we incarnate for a purpose comes from a childhood dream I still remember to this day. In the dream – I was there (not in my body) and my being was absorbing by looking out into what seemed to be a vast expanse of nothingness. I could vaguely perceive shapes and lights and yet somehow I understood that in the expanse there was life continuing in some form but there was no clear image; it seemed otherworldly. I sensed an entity beside me impressing me with conversation about the journey I was to take into this vastness. The knowing that I was to go was within me and I was afraid, I wanted to stay right where I was amidst beauty and comfort. The entity beside me felt full of wisdom, a Master Teacher or Sage perhaps; I was being impressed with words of assurance, yet at the same time being impressed with the knowing that I must go. Our conversation was not verbal; it was through thoughts transferring soul to soul. The entity showed me a journey of twists turns and hurdles to manage as I lived this path. I felt such anxiousness about this strange adventure. The entity explained that as I journeyed I would always be moving toward the light, I could barely see its glow off in the distance. In that space of time I understood that I was supposed to go because going was part of my destiny, my life plan, my personal journey. Now the knowing embraced me and I awoke.

This was a continuing dream for many years. As I turned toward a spiritual path and became more enlightened I came to the understanding that we incarnate with a purpose and part of the journey is working our way through to complete our purpose. This is not pre-destination. This is something we chose to experience for soul growth. It may be our own personal soul growth and it could be incarnating in groups or to participate in the growth of another soul.

Was my dream only a dream or was it a soul memory of before birth? Does it even matter? In my heart, my soul remembers the time before being born here on earth – my soul remembers the trepidation, anxiety, even fear I felt at leaving my original home and braving this world. I admit I may have anxiety about how I will die but I've always known deep within that I was going to live this earthly life for a while – then when I reach the glow of the light at the end of my journey, I get to return to my original home and be blessed for the experiences.

MEDIUMSHIP

Mediumship is about communicating with spirit entities and proving the continuity of life. Everything is energy and vibration. The energies of the medium and spirit entity must engage for this marvelous experience of spirit communication to happen. The humanness of the medium operates at a much lower rate of vibration than spirit. Therefore the medium through meditation must learn to raise his/her vibration while the communicating spirits must lower their vibration. The process of connecting is one of the reasons a medium cannot always connect with a certain spirit while another medium might be able to connect. Spirit entities must also learn the process of communicating and the entity may simply not yet know how to communicate. Spiritualists do not believe spirit entities are idle for eternity. Spiritualists believe that here is service work on all levels of existence so who you want to specifically communicate with might be busy elsewhere.

I was taught to test the spirits when receiving a message. There should be something within the message such as a description, a memory, a favorite item, any bit of information that confirms to the receiver that *yes* this is definitely so and so (I call this simply the key because it helps me unlock the message). Just like the licorice candy my husband presented there will be a memory connection that you will recognize as proof. When receiving a message by a medium there may be times you might not recognize the spirit entity right away; generally the identity will simply come to you later or you might have to ask a family member or friend if they recognize the memory or description.

Mediums work with what we call spirit teachers and guides. They are there to help us through our life journey and some will stay with us and others will come for specific purposes. When mediums receive messages from spirit entities they are working with and through their guides. Our guides keep us from being overwhelmed with the energies of spirits so desperately wanting to communicate; our guides work as our buffer. Mediums and their guides are a team and message work is definitely a team effort. Our guides and teachers are also there for us whenever we need assistance and all that we have to do is ask.

Mediumship is connecting with spirit entities. When a message is received about future events, it is how the communicating spirit entity sees that event is going to play out in that moment. If any shift is made, the outcome changes by our own choices and actions. The possibilities in our lives are limitless and so are the outcomes. Since we have free will and are working with thoughts, words, actions and deeds in creating our own future, when receiving a message from spirit, they relay one possible scenario that is seen by the communicating spirit at that time. This means a medium cannot guarantee the message received by a spirit entity will play out exactly as perceived during a reading.

I have come to realize that time is man-made and in the spirit realms time does not have the same relevance as on the earth plane. The relevance portion of the message is the event. If the spirit relays a message about Easter it might not be next Easter it might be any future Easter. Just because a message is seen as a possible scenario, always remember you have choice and any action you take is your responsibility, and may impact the predicted event. What I do when I receive a message of the future, I wait until it starts playing out then and only then do I decide whether to act. I always give thanks for the hint from the Universe about this event.

I have on several occasions received messages from mediums about events that made absolutely no sense to me at the time. For instance, I received a message about watching my step because they saw me stepping off a very low deck and getting injured; I went to a friend's house and she greeted me at the door with a cast on her leg. She had built a deck which was maybe a foot off the ground and she had accidently stepped off the edge. Spirit can relay messages that are not directly about you but the message can be regarding the people around you such as friends, family, co-workers, etc.

When we leave this earthly existence and go back to the Spirit Realms, we still are who we are retaining our personality and all our learning experiences. Spirits do not necessarily become all knowing just because they have shed their physical body. Spirits can give us guidance and advice by requesting their assistance. But advice is only advice, we are responsible for the choices and actions taken from the advice received from any entity. A medium can relay a message but he/she is relaying information. You take the message and whatever action is your choice.

Do I see ghosts? On occasion yes, I have seen spirit manifest but mostly I sense or feel spirit around me and the spirit impresses me with information. The impression may be like visions or pictures or I may be impressed with words similar to a telepathic conversation. I have on occasions heard my name audibly called and raps on doors. Needless to say, I have investigated these occurrences to be sure there was no other explanation except spirit activity. Once my husband was with me and we both heard independent voice phenomena; my husband was a skeptic and when he heard this voice seemly come out of the air he was stunned to say the least.

ENERGY CIRCLES

I was not a child prodigy and I did not always communicate with spirit entities. Growing up I did not even know about mediums or spirit communication. I was taught how to unfold or bring forth my ability to communicate with spirits by a qualified teacher and by reading all the books I could find on the subject. Anyone can learn to open up to become aware of spirits and to communicate with them. Every medium develops a gift for spirit communication; the most noted are clairvoyance (clear seeing), clairaudience (clear hearing) and clairsentience (clear sensing). Through a steady practice of meditation I learned to raise my vibration preparing my physical being for spirit communication.

I have found the best format for unfolding mediumship is what we at our church call Energy Circles. In this type of format it does not matter if you are a beginner or have been communicating with spirit for years, all levels of experienced participants are learning from each other. This has proven to be a no stress way for mediums to unfold and all mediums to use their gift. We form a circle of positive energy drawing in spirit loved ones who wish to communicate. The circle always starts with discussion about mediumship or any spiritual topic, followed by a prayer, meditation, and then everyone in the circle is given the opportunity to give and receive messages. Our opening prayer invites spirit teachers and loved ones to join our circle; with a request for protection asking that only good will come into our circle.

What I relay to individuals who are unfolding in our circle is that, the process is like stepping into attunement; in the beginning it may feel like a shift of energy. I started by becoming aware of how I felt when I gave a message from a spirit loved one and the message was confirmed. This feeling was how I learned to recognize that my vibration was high enough to communicate with spirit. Then I used this memory to make a conscious shift into my place of attunement where I comfortably felt I was in sync with the higher vibratory rate for spirit communication. In the beginning it was a very profound feeling; it was almost like a physical shift.

Gradually I became confident enough that I made this shift without conscious knowledge, it was a natural phenomenon just like taking a breath.

When the circle begins to wane, the circle is closed with prayer and a statement to close our spirit channels unless an emergency or need arises until the next appointed time. There is lots of discussion on the opening and closing of channels; however, I was taught that I came to live an earth experience and so I do not keep my channels open all the time. For me it's a process of shifting into attunement to connect with spirit when required or desired. If there is a need or emergency my spirit team finds a way to warn me. I have been saved from car accidents on more than one occasion.

SPIRITUAL HEALING

Mediumship used in spiritual healing is about attuning to those in the Spirit Realms who serve as healers for and through our Higher Power. We, trained healers are serving as a channel or instrument for the healing energy of the Infinite Spirit. Healing is always requested for the individuals highest and best. All healings come from Infinite Spirit. It makes no difference if the healing is brought about by physical methods or if it is spiritual healing brought about by spirit, healing is an action of the Natural Laws that govern all facets of our lives.

What is spiritual healing? Spiritual healing involves the connection from Infinite Spirit to the spirit helpers working with Natural Law to the healer working with spirit entities to direct healing energies to the recipient. The healer is serving as a channel for these healing energies. Spiritual healing is for the whole being (body, mind and spirit). Spiritual healing enhances understanding of the continuity of life. Spiritual healing renews awareness and connection to Infinite Spirit. One essential fact of healing work is attunement or establishing a state of affinity with spirit helpers. This attunement is a coming together of our spiritual selves and the energies necessary for healing to occur.

A prayer that is used in Spiritualist services is this Healing Prayer taken from the National Spiritualist Association of Churches website (www.NSAC.org).

I Ask The Great Unseen Healing Force
To Remove All Obstructions
From My Mind And Body
And To Restore Me To Perfect Health.
I Ask This In All Sincerity And Honesty,
And I Will Do My Part.

I Ask This Great Unseen Healing Force
To Help Both Present And Absent Ones
Who Are In Need Of Help
And To Restore Them To Perfect Health.

I Put My Trust In The Love And Power Of God.

NATURAL LAW

What if someone said to you "Open a gate into the unknown and you will find everything you need to know about life and how you can live the life you desire; would you take the challenge"? I was struggling through life feeling like I was mostly banging my head against a brick wall when through Spiritualism I learned there is a flow to the way the Universe operates and we can tap into that flow making life so much easier. This flow of operation is the laws Infinite Spirit set into motion in the beginning called Natural Law or Universal Law. Understanding and working with these laws is how we co-create the life we desire.

There is an abundance of Natural Laws. There is an abundance of books on Natural Law ("The Laws of Spirit" by Dan Millman is one of my favorites); and there are numerous classes on working with the laws offering guidance in various methods in manifesting your desires. What I embraced about Natural Law is once you grasp the way the Universe works and keep in the flow of its operation, life is less complex. We co-create with the Infinite Spirit through our thoughts, words, actions and deeds. Everything is energy, we are energy so to manifest our desire we work with energy.

The law we read about the most is "like attracts like" or the Law of Attraction. When I work with the Law of Attraction I set my intent about what exactly it is that I desire to manifest. Then I think of something or an event that puts me in the mood of love or great joy which builds high positive energy within me. I write my intent and I also speak it out into the atmosphere. Now it is time to trust and keep *me* out of the way and let the Universe do the magic of creating. I always ask that this be done in the highest and best manner. The central key here is to believe beyond any doubt that this will be; then thank Infinite Spirit and live as if it has already happened.

Think about the Physical Law of Gravity. It works because Infinite Spirit set it into operation. The law continues to operate without any conscious thought on our part. We simply trust that we will not float out into the great beyond. If we can trust that gravity will hold us onto the earth because Infinite Spirit made it so then we take this trust into all areas of our life when working with Natural Laws.

Where we get ourselves into problems is for instance, the Spiritual Law of Integrity. In any given situation what would you do if no one else would ever know; would you act the same as you do when you feel accountable. The truth is you are accountable. The Law of Integrity says you believe in right living and do so under all circumstances. When this operation does not happen then within you distrust is created because you know you did not always live the Law of Integrity. Now you question whether others are being truthful or honest with you. You have created an energy field of distrust around you so now you are likely to experience more situations matching your own state of distrust.

Working with Natural Law does not absolve us from experiences but it sure makes getting through experiences less stressful. It's about trust and belief like the Law of Gravity. We simply know and believe there is gravity. Trust that Universal Laws are always in operation, work with them and believe.

SYNCHRONICITY

My first exposure to synchronicity came from a small book "When God Winks" by SQuire Rushnell (I highly recommend this book). I learned how when you paid attention to the signals or signs provided by the Universe, these signs give you guidance. The signs could be as simple as thinking of a question then turning on the radio or TV and voila your answer.

Even though I didn't know or understand synchronicity, it is what led me to Spiritualism. When I was a teenager I read the book "The Story of Edgar Cayce; There is a river…" by Thomas Sugrue. Years passed and a friend talked me into going for a psychic reading. More years passed and a friend talked me into visiting yet another psychic. The years go by then through my workplace I became friends with a woman who introduced me to friend of hers who was a medium. (Are you noticing all the hints I am receiving and ignoring throughout my life?) This medium told me of a Spiritualist Church close by where I finally attended a psychic fair. At the fair I told the reader I wanted to learn how to connect with spirit; I wanted to do what she was doing. About the same time my significant other introduced me to his brother's girlfriend who was a Spiritualist and she invited me to start attending church with her. All of these events were stepping stones to who I am today! Not all synchronistic events take years in a lifetime to follow, most are hints or answers to daily dilemmas.

There is a lot of jargon about what is synchronicity; to me it's simply guidance. When seemingly random unexplained events happen one after another which are notable, then I take the hint and follow it through. Just like spirit messages there always seems to be a key that lets me know it's a hint from Infinite Spirit and pay attention. Ask for this guidance and it will come.

PRAYER

Divine Intervention comes from all of our prayers which are heard as energy and these thought forms are creating what is in our highest and best interest. As a Spiritualist I know we co-create with our Infinite Spirit so we can change our environment through our own thoughts, words, actions and deeds. All change comes from within so when we pray we must make the changes within so that our desire will manifest.

A good way to know how many prayers we send out into space is to write them down. I wrote down my prayers for over a year. One day I decided to read my prayer journey and I was amazed how many prayers there were and I was more impressed with how many prayers were answered. I found that once a prayer was answered I had moved onto the next one and forgot about the last crisis or need or desire. In reading my prayer journal I found I had been blessed with answered prayers all year.

My understanding about prayer is that we cannot and do not have the right to change or interfere in another's life path or lessons to suit our desires for them. This is an area where divine guidance plays the most important role – there is a trust that everything is in divine order. We can pray for another asking for the highest and best. We can pray that good comes to the one we are praying for giving them guidance and understanding to help them. I have prayed that a mentor come into someone's life to help them find direction and purpose.

Prayer is a trust in the everlasting flow of love emitting from Infinite Spirit. Prayer is about asking for the best possible outcome then trusting and letting go. This is a hard task when someone you care about is ill, or when the rent's due and you don't know where the money is coming from; or your children keep banging their heads against the same wall and you can't get them to see the light! Living the action of trust and confidence that there are blessings in disguise in every situation brings about a shift to the positive. This shift is actually coming from within you. When you shift to positive thoughts, words, actions and deeds then you have changed; now you can draw to you the positive things in your life your desire. Allow yourself to recognize the *kn*owing deep within your gut that the Universe is working on the best plan is our only sure bet for a good outcome.

Prayer is communication with your Higher Power. I do have special prayers I say but when I send prayers into the heavens; I am having conversation with Infinite Spirit and I know the Universe receives and knows my heart's desire. This communication with Infinite Spirit can be through body language, spoken words, thoughts, any form of feeling being emitted at the time. Communication is vibration. When I serve as a medium I will ask for the sound of your voice because then I can feel your vibratory rate I can hone into individual energies. I do not ask for the sound of Infinite Spirit's voice. What I do is bring into my heart the highest vibratory rate known to man which is the energy of love. Then I release it into the universal space trusting that my prayers are received because Infinite Spirit is love in its highest form and all of us are connected in this energy.

BOOKS AND CLASSES

Books abound in our world and what blessings books have been for me. I currently have around 100 books on my electronic book device. Prior to digital books I donated books and bookshelves to our church that I had accumulated to make them available for others to read. Books are a means to fuel our belief system. There are books that feed your core beliefs, others that you instantly feel this is not for me, and some you will only resonate with a few pages then discard the remainder. All of this is okay; it is part of our learning process, designing our own beliefs. I once had an experience of a book falling off the shelf in a bookstore it took me three hits before I took the hint and bought the book. I am grateful for all those people who chose to share their experiences and stories. The books I have read throughout my spiritual growth have helped me be who I am today.

Classes are important; sharing questions and thoughts; basically being with like minds is essential to spiritual growth. I do not mean that without classes you cannot become enlightened. With classes there is guidance from teachers who can offer understanding of all you are feeling and advise you of any pitfalls they may have experienced. Even though I have been a Spiritualist for over twenty years and I am a credentialed NSAC Teacher I still attend classes. If I did not attend classes, I would not have new knowledge or understanding to share. Spiritual growth is not something you do for a while then it's completed. Its evolution, we are constantly evolving to higher states of consciousness. Classes are like books. Some you will resonate with and others maybe not so much. All will allow you to grow through the experiences. Search for what resonates with you!

GRATITUDE

Always give thanks! Gratitude is energy and has a frequency of love and thankfulness. When we take time to be grateful and appreciate our life journey; we are drawing more things to be grateful for into our energy field. When I spend my days in an attitude of gratitude I seem to stay in the flow of positivity and goodness. Gratitude is about big and small things. I give thanks for a good parking space wherever I go, so now my family knows that if I'm in the car there will be a spot close to the door. In our toughest of times when we face challenges there are reasons to give thanks.

Gratitude is also about finding the blessings in disguise within any turmoil. I had three family members in two different hospitals all at the same time. The two hospitals were not even close to each other. Of course I tell Infinite Spirit this is impossible that I need a workable plan! I was on my way to stay with the family member at the farthest hospital when I got a call that she was being released. I immediately gave thanks! I changed routes to the other hospital when I arrived I found the other two family members were at opposite ends of the same hall. I paused and gave thanks for the workable plan at that moment. Had I stayed in a stress mode over what I perceived as a seemingly impossible situation what I would have received was more stress. When I shifted my consciousness to knowing there was help and believing it would be so, then being grateful for the plan I shifted from stress to flow and it was doable.

If I have someone or a situation where I have concerns, I shift my consciousness and I simply give thanks for Infinite Spirit handling that situation for me. I believe in gratitude energy which is loving the outcome before it happens, staying out of the way of the positivity, and not continuing my worry wheel where I go round and round getting nowhere. Gratitude is being thankful for all that you have and all that you are yet to receive in everyday moments.

HOW ONE PERSON MAKES A DIFFERENCE

I believe one person can make a difference by raising their vibration and releasing the higher energy out into the world. It is not at all that daunting of a feat. It's about taking care of yourself and your space. When I am living a spiritual path my life is working for me and I can guarantee that others will notice. They will notice and they will question and they will want their life to work as well as they see mine is working for me. So it starts with self then the next person then the next person on and on until spiritual living has spread like an epidemic throughout humanity. All of these inspired people are raising the vibration and shifting the mass consciousness to higher levels.

I serve as a volunteer Pastor at The Spiritualist Church of Indianapolis (www.TSCOI.org). I work with dedicated people who volunteer their time who make sharing the Science, Religion and Philosophy of Spiritualism possible. As a medium I do not do private readings. There are many wonderful readers already and that was not the direction I felt was right for me; I serve as a medium in my church service work. I often serve as a medium for non-profit organizations at fundraising events. Our church family gathers clothing, food and other goods to help those in our community who are in need. Many in our church family volunteer their services for non-profit organizations that they are passionate about. Every act of kindness makes a difference. Spend your day smiling and raise the vibration of all those who come in contact with you. Share the love and light of Infinite Spirit with the world – that is our true service work.

CONCLUSION

Spiritualism has a rich and colorful history. Starting with the Fox Sisters whose ability to communicate with a murdered peddler sparked the movement toward Modern American Spiritualism. The Spiritualist pioneers dedicated their life to bringing public attention to the Science, Philosophy and Religion of Spiritualism. The data collected on the phenomena of mediumship proving that death is only of the physical body is a part of our archived history. We are spirit, we are eternal beings! I started my studies reading the NSAC Spiritualist Manual, and thus my journey of learning began. It took me years but eventually I enrolled in the Morris Pratt Institute's (MPI) full course studies for ordination. I recommend visiting the websites of www.NSAC.org and www.MPI.org; also be sure to check out their bookstores.

What I hope I accomplished in these few pages is to offer understanding about Spiritualism through my life experiences and ignite your plucky curiosity. I want to reiterate that we are all interconnected and we come from the same Source – Infinite Spirit. Most of all I hope I unlocked your mind to the boundless possibilities. Please seek churches, books and classes for spiritual growth and enlightenment. I am who I am today because of my journey of learning and I reserve the right to grow beyond what I believe now because I'm a work in progress always changing, always learning, always evolving toward higher consciousness.

NATIONAL SPIRITUALIST ASSOCIATION OF CHURCHES' SPIRITUALISM

Definitions of Spiritualism from the NSAC Spiritualist Manual:

Spiritualism Is a Science because it investigates, analyzes and classifies facts and manifestations demonstrated from the spirit side of life.

Spiritualism Is a Philosophy because it studies the Laws of Nature both on the seen and unseen sides of life and bases its conclusions upon present observed facts. It accepts statements of observed facts of past ages and conclusions drawn therefrom, when sustained by reason and results of observed facts of the present day.

Spiritualism Is a Religion because it strives to understand and to comply with the Physical, Mental and Spiritual Laws of Nature, which are the laws of

God.

The Spiritualist Declaration of Principles taken from the NSAC Spiritualist Manual are not creed or dogma, these Principles are our basic beliefs.

1. We believe in Infinite Intelligence.

2. We believe that the phenomena of nature, both physical and spiritual, are the expression of Infinite Intelligence.

3. We affirm that a correct understanding of such expression and living in accordance therewith constitute true religion.

4. We affirm that the existence and personal identity of the individual continue after the change called death.

5. We affirm that communication with the so-called dead is a fact, scientifically proven by the phenomena of Spiritualism.

6. We believe that the highest morality is contained in the Golden Rule: "Do unto others as you would have them do unto you."

7. We affirm the moral responsibility of the individual and that we make our own happiness or unhappiness as we obey or disobey Nature's Physical and Spiritual Laws.

8. We affirm that the doorway to reformation is never closed against any soul here or hereafter.

9. We affirm that the Precepts of Prophecy and Healing are Divine attributes proven through Mediumship.

NSAC Simplified Declaration of Principles:

1. We believe in God.

2. We believe that God is expressed through all of nature.

3. True religion is living in obedience to Nature's Laws.

4. We never die.

5. Spiritualism proves that we can talk with people in the Spirit World.

6. Be kind, do good, and others will do likewise.

7. We bring unhappiness to ourselves by the errors we make and we will be happy if we obey the laws of life.

8. Every day is a new beginning.

9. Prophecy and healing are expressions of God.

The symbol of Spiritualism is the sunflower; Spiritualism's motto is:

"As the sunflower turns its face toward the light of the sun, so Spiritualism turns the face of humanity toward the light of truth."

BIBLIOGRAPHY

Jefts Rev. Lena Barnes Pamphlets [Book]. – Lily Dale : Distributed by the National Spiritualist Association of Churches, Inc..

Millman Dan The Laws of Spirit; A Tale of Transformation [Book]. - Tiburon : H J Kramer Inc., 1995.

National Spiritualist Association of Churches, Inc. NSAC Spiritualist Manual [Book]. - Lily Dale : [s.n.], 1998

Praagh James Van Talking to Heaven A Medium's Message of Life After Death [Book]. - New York : Penguin Group, 1997

Rushnell Squire When God Winks [Book]. – Hillsboro : Beyond Words Publishing, Inc., 2001

Shakuntala Modi M.D. Memories of God and Creation; Remembering from the Subconscious Mind [Book]. - Charlottesville : Hampton Roads Publishing Company, Inc., 2000.

Sugrue Thomas The Story of Edgar Cayce; There is a river…" [Book]. - New York : Henry Holt and Company, Inc., 1942, 1945

RECOMMENDED WEBSITES

www.TSCOI.org
The Spiritualist Church of Indianapolis

www.NSAC.org
National Spiritualist Association of Churches, Inc.

www.MPI.org
Morris Pratt Institute

www.ingramcontent.com/pod-product-compliance
Lightning Source LLC
Chambersburg PA
CBHW060949050426
42337CB00052B/3290